NAMING BABY

NAMING BABY

*The Answer To Every Parent's
Christening Problem*

BY

EUGENE STONE

WARD LOCK LIMITED · LONDON

© *Ward Lock Limited 1954*

Reprinted 1970
Reprinted 1972

ISBN 0 7063 1051 9

PREFACE

NAMING BABY can be a very long, hazardous and trying business, for there are almost as many difficulties to overcome as, say, at a Four-Power Conference. For example, will Baby in later years thank or curse the appellation so painstakingly arrived at; will it please the grandparents—a point for the most careful diplomacy; is the sound in sympathy with the surname; is it pretentious and difficult to pronounce; has it a diminutive which is not at all complimentary; and so on and so on. Nevertheless all difficult tasks repay the care and devotion lavished on them—not least NAMING BABY.

This little book, of course, does not attempt to solve these multitudinous problems for they are essentially personal. However, it is the compiler's hope that it will serve to aid in this onerous task by showing what a great variety of names there are to choose from, and something of their origin and meaning.

To save space the following abbreviations have been used: (b) for boy, (g) for girl, q.v. for look see, *con.* for contraction and *dim.* for diminutive.

Should the reader be tempted to go further into the fascinating world of names, then he or she would be well advised first to consult, *The Oxford Dictionary of English Christian Names* by E. G. Withycombe, *Jack and Jill* by Ernest Weekley and *Name This Child* by Eric Partridge.

A

ANNE

Abner (b) Hebrew; 'father of light'.

Abraham (b) Hebrew; 'father of a multitude. A most appropriate name for the great Patriarch and America's best known President.

Abigail (g) Hebrew; 'a father's joy'.

Absalom (b) Hebrew; 'father of peace'.

Achilles (b) Greek; 'he without lips'. Name of the Homeric hero who vanquished Hector (Iliad).

Ada (g) Teutonic; meaning and origin obscure, but thought to mean 'happy'. A very popular name in Victorian days.

Adam (b) Hebrew; 'man'. Derived from Adamah, 'red earth'.

Adela (g) Teutonic; 'noble'. Fashionable with the Victorians.

Adelaide (g) Teutonic; 'noble kind'. Name of the popular wife of William IV.

Adeline (g) Teutonic; another derivative from 'noble' *Con.* ALINE.

Adrian (b) Latin; 'of the Adriatic; black'.

Adriana, Adrienne (g) Latin and French feminine forms of ADRIAN.

Agatha (g) Greek; 'good'.

Agnes (g) Greek; 'pure'. One of the four great virgin

5

saints. Poetically immortalised in Keats' "The Eve of St. Agnes".

Allen, Allan, Alan (b) Celtic. Meaning obscure.

Alaric (b) Old German; 'ruler of all'.

Alastair, Allister (b) Scottish contraction of the Greek ALEXANDER. Many forms of spelling are found.

Albert (b) Old German; 'nobly bright'. Popularised in the nineteenth century by the Prince Consort.

Alberta (g) Feminine version of the above.

Alexander (b) Greek; 'defender of men'. Known to all because of the titanic exploits of the Macedonian king of that name. *Dim.* ALEX, ALEC. *Con.* ALEXIS.

Alexandra (g) Feminine counterpart of the above. Popularised by the wife of Edward VII. Other forms are ALEXANDRINA, ALEXIA. *Dim.* ALEX, SANDRA, LEXY.

Alfred (b) Teutonic; 'elf-counsel'. Made famous by the early English king of that name. *Dim.* ALF.

Algernon (b) Old French; 'bewhiskered'. *Dim.* ALGY.

Alice (g) O. German; 'truth'. Also ALICIA, ALISA and other spellings. *Con.* ALISON (Scottish). A popular Victorian name.

Alwyn, Aylwyn (b) Teutonic; 'noble friend'.

Amabel(la) (g) Latin; 'lovable'.

Amanda (g) Latin; 'fit to be loved'. *Dim.* MANDA, MANDY.

Amaryllis (g) Greek; 'refreshing stream'. Formerly a popular pastoral name.

Ambrose (b) Greek; 'immortal'.

Amy (g) French; 'loved'. Sometimes spelt AIMEE.

Anastasia (g) Greek; 'one who shall rise again'. *Con.* ANSTICE. *Dim.* ANTY, STASIA.

Andrea (g) Italian; feminine form of ANDREW, q.v.

Andrew (b) Greek; 'manly'. Mainly found in Scotland, because of the patron saint of that name.

Aneurin (b) Welsh; 'truly golden'.

Angela (g) Greek; contraction of ANGELICA, q.v.

Angelica (g) Greek; 'angelic one'. ANGELINA is a variant of this christian name.

Anne, Ann, Anna, Annie, Hannah (g) Hebrew; 'grace'. *Dim.* ANITA, ANNETTE, NAN, NANETTE, NANCY. JOHANNAH was the original form from which the others were derived, together with JOHN and its derivatives.

Anselm (b) Teutonic; 'divine helmet'. Popularised on the continent by the eleventh century bishop of that name.

Anthea (g) Greek; 'lady of flowers'.

Anthony, Antony (b) Latin; 'inestimable'. Two saints and the famous triumvir have made this name popular *Dim.* TONY.

Antonia, Antoinette (g) Latin and French feminine forms of Anthony.

April, Averil (g) The name of the month.

Arabella (g) Scottish; 'yielding to prayer'. *Dim.* BELLA, BELLE.

Archibald (b) Teutonic; 'nobly bold'. *Dim.* ARCHIE.

Arnold (b) Teutonic; 'strong as the eagle'.

Arthur (b) Anglo-Saxon; 'valorous'. Made known through the Celtic legend of King Arthur and the Knights of the Round Table. *Dim.* ARTIE, ART.

Astra (g) Greek; 'starlike'.

Astrid (g) O. German; 'God's, or divine, strength'.

Aubrey (b) Old German; 'fairy king'. Has its roots in Oberon, traditional name of the king of the fairies.

Audrey (g) Anglo-Saxon; 'noble might'. A contraction of ETHELDREDA.

Augustus (b) Latin; 'majestic'. *Dim.* AUGUSTINE, of which AUSTIN is a contraction.

Augusta (g) Latin; feminine form of the above.

Avis (g) Latin; 'a bird'.

Aylmer (b) Anglo-Saxon; 'nobly famous'. Common in America in the form of ELMER.

B

BORIS

Baldwin (b) Teutonic; 'bold friend'.

Barbara (g) Latin; 'the stranger'. The name of one of the great virgin saints of the Roman Catholic Church. *Dim.* BARBIE, BABETTE, BABS, BAR, etc.

Barnabas, Barnaby (b) Hebrew; 'son of exhortation'. *Dim.* BARNEY.

Barry (b) Celtic; 'looking straight at the mark'.

Bartholomew (b) Hebrew; 'son of the furrows'. *Dim.* BART, BARTIE. *Con.* BARTLET, BARTLEY, BARTLEMY, of which BARTLE is a diminutive.

Basil (b) Greek; 'a king'. Popularised by Keats' poem "The Pot of Basil".

Beatrice, Beatrix (g) Latin; 'joy-giver; blessed'. Beatrice was made known by Dante. *Dim.* BEA, BEAT, BEATIE, TRIXIE.

Belinda (g) Old German; 'serpent-like'.

Benedict (b) Latin; 'blessed'. *Con.* BENNET.

Benjamin (b) Hebrew; 'son of the right hand'. *Dim.* BEN, BENJIE, BENNIE.

Berenice, Bernice (g) Greek; 'bringing victory'.

Bernard, Barnard (b) German; 'having the courage of a bear'. *Dim.* BERNIE.

Bernarda, Bernadina, Bernadette (g) Feminine form of the above.

Bertha (g) Teutonic; 'the bright one'.

Bertram, Bertrand, Bartram (b) Teutonic; 'bright raven'.

Beryl (g) Greek; the name of a jewel.

Bevan, Bevin (b) Celtic; 'son of the young warrior'. Frequently found as a surname.

Bianca (f) Italian; 'white'.

Blanche (g) French; 'white'. *Dim.* BLANCHARDINE.

Bonamy (b) French; 'good friend' and is a literal translation of *bon ami*.

Boniface (b) Latin; 'well-doer'.

Bonita (g) Latin; 'good'.

*➤ **Boris** (b) Russian; 'warrior'.

Boyd (b) Celtic; 'yellow-hair'. Still used but more often found as a surname.

Bran (b) Celtic; 'raven'.

Brand (b) Scandinavian; 'a flame'.

Brenda (g) Feminine form of the above. Quite popular with stage and film stars.

*✳ **Brandon, Brendon** (b) Celtic; 'dweller near the beacon'.

Brian, Bryan (b) Celtic; 'strength'. Popular in Ireland because of the tenth century king, Brian Boru.

Brice, Bryce (b) Probably of Celtic origin and said to mean 'swift' or 'speedy'.

Bridget, Bridgit, Brigid, Brighid (g) Celtic; 'strength'. The name of a Celtic goddess and then of one of the Irish saints. *Dim.* BRIDE, BRIDIE, BIDDY, BIRDIE.

Bronwen (g) Celtic; 'white-breasted'. A common name in Wales.

Bruce (b) Old French; meaning obscure. Since the thirteenth century used chiefly in Scotland, and name of Robert the Bruce.

Brunhild, Brunhilda (g) Norse; 'brown battle-maid'. Made known in this country chiefly through Wagner's opera, *The Ring*.

*➤ **Bruno** (b) German; 'brown'.

Bunty (g) There is no etymology for this name, originally the pet-name for lambs from their habit of "bunting" or "butting".

C

CYRIL

Cadwallader (b) Welsh; 'battle-arranger'.

Caesar (b) Latin; 'hairy'. The name was common in Rome two hundred years before Julius Caesar, and owes its fame to the many famous members of the Caesar family, of which Julius was but one.

Caleb (b) Hebrew; 'bold'. More popular in America.

Calvin (b) Latin; 'bald'. Associated with the great protestant reformer of that name in the sixteenth century.

Camilla (g) Latin; 'attendant at a sacrifice'. Very popular in England after the Reformation.

Candace (g) Latin; originally a dynastic title of Ethiopian queens. Popular in America. *Dim.* CANDY.

Cara (g) Celtic; 'friend'. and equally:
  Italian; 'dear'.

Caradoc (b) Celtic; 'beloved'.

Carlo (b) Italian; 'man'.

Carmel, Carmela (g) Hebrew; 'vineyard'.

Carol (b) Origin uncertain; probably from the same root as Charles.

Carola (g) Feminine form of the above.

Caroline, Carolina (g) Feminine counterpart of CHARLES, q.v. Popularised by the English queen of that name. *Dim.* CARRIE, CAROL.

Cassandra (g) Greek; 'helper of men'. Associated with Cassandra, daughter of Priam of Troy, who had the gift of prophecy. *Dim*. CASSIE.

Catherine, Catherina (g) Greek; 'pure'. Also spelt with a K. *Con*. KATHLEEN (Irish) KATRINE (English). *Dim*. KATE, KATY, CATHIE, KAY, KITTY, KIT.

Cecil (b) Latin; 'blind'.

Cecilia, Cecily (g) Feminine form of the above and name of St. Cecilia, virgin martyr and patron saint of music. *Dim*. CISSIE.

Cedric (b) Celtic; 'chieftain'. *Dim*. CEDIE.

Celia (g) Latin; 'heavenly'. Popular with the pastoral and lyric poets of the seventeenth and eighteenth centuries.

Charissa, Charis (g) Greek; 'love'.

Charity (g) Greek; 'love'. *Con*. CHERRY, CHATTY.

Charles (b) Teutonic; 'a man'. One of the most popular boys' names. A favourite royal name in France and England. *Dim*. CHARLIE.

Charlotte (g) French feminine equivalent of the above. Made popular in England by the wife of George III. *Dim*. LOTTIE.

Charmian (g) Greek; 'source of charm'.

Chloe (g) Greek; 'green, summery'. Originally owed its popularity to the myth of "Daphnis and Chloe", but in America came to be associated with negresses.

Christabel (g) Latin; 'beautiful anointed one'. Popularised in the early nineteenth century by Coleridge's unfinished poem.

Christian (b and g) Latin; 'follower of Christ'. For girls it is sometimes spelt CHRISTIANA. *Dim*. CHRIS, CHRISTY.

Christina, Christine (g) Feminine diminutives of the Latin CHRISTUS, 'the anointed'. *Dim*. CHRISTIE, CHRISSIE, CHRIS, TINA, TEENY.

Christopher (b) Greek; 'bearer of Christ'. St. Christopher was the patron saint of travellers. *Dim*. KIT, CHRIS.

Chrystal, Crystal (g) One of the jewel-names.

Ciprian, Cyprian (b) Latin; 'inhabitant of Cyprus'.

Clair, Clare (b) Latin; 'illustrious'.

Clara, Clare (g) Latin; feminine form of the above. Originated by St. Clare, a follower of St. Francis.

Clarence (b) Latin; 'being renowned'. *Dim.* CLARE.

Clarice, Clarissa (g) Derivatives of the above. *Dim.* CLARRIE.

Claud, Claude (g) Latin; 'lame'. Originally made famous by the Roman Emperor Claudius.

Claudia, Claudine (g) Latin and French feminine forms of the above.

Clement (b) Latin; 'merciful'. *Dim.* CLEM.

Clemence, Clemency (g) Feminine forms of the above Other forms are CLEMENTINE, CLEMENTIA, CLEMENTINA *Dig.* CLEMMIE.

Cleopatra (g) Greek; 'fame of the father'. Popularised by Queen Cleopatra of Egypt, famous for her beauty and her disastrous love affairs with Caesar and Mark Anthony *Dim.* CLEO.

Clifford (b) Teutonic; 'dweller on a slope'. *Dim.* CLIFF.

Clive (b) Contraction of the above, but owes its greater popularity to Clive of India.

Clothilde, Clothilda (g) Latin; 'famous battlemaid'.

Colin (b) Latin; 'a dove'.

Conrad (b) Teutonic; 'bold speech'. *Dim.* CON.

Constance (g) Latin; 'firm of purpose'. Also found as CONSTANTIA. *Dim.* CONNIE.

Constantine (b) Originally a masculine diminutive of the above, made famous by the Roman Emperor of that name.

Cora, Corinna (g) Greek; 'maiden'.

Coralie (g) French adaption of the above.

Cordelia (g) Celtic; 'daughter of the sea'. Owes its popularity almost entirely to the character of that name in Shakespeare's "King Lear".

Cornelia (g) Latin; 'regal'.

Cornelius (b) Masculine equivalent of the above.

Cosmo (b) Latin; 'universe'.

Crispin, Crispian (b) Latin; 'curly-haired'.

Curtis (b) Middle English; 'short hose'; or Old French 'courteous'.

Cuthbert (b) Anglo-Saxon; 'famous splendour'.

Cymbeline (b) Celtic; 'lord of the sun'.

Cynthia (g) Greek; another name for ARTEMIS or DIANA. A favourite name in England with the pastoral poets.

Cyril (b) Greek; 'lordly'.

D

DORCAS

Dagmar (g) Danish; 'Dane's joy', not common in England.

Daisy (g) Anglo-Saxon; 'eye of day', and not a pet-name for MARGARET.

Damian (b) Greek; 'tamer'.

Daniel (b) Hebrew; 'judged of God'. Now very popular in Ireland. *Dim.* DAN, DANNY.

Daphne (g) Greek; 'bay-tree'. The original mythological Daphne was turned into a bay-tree to escape from Apollo.

Darcy (b) Irish; 'dweller in the stronghold'.

Darrell, Daryl (b) Anglo-Saxon; derives from 'darling'.

David (b) Hebrew; 'beloved'. Name of the patron saint of Wales, and one of the most popular boys' names. *Dim.* DAVE, DAVY.

Dawn (g) A literal translation of AURORA, the dawn. A modern name.

Deborah (g) Hebrew; 'eloquent'. *Dim.* DEBBY, DEB.

Decimus (b) Latin; 'the tenth child'. *Con.* DECIUS.

Decima (g) Feminine equivalent of the above.

13

Deirdre (g) Celtic; 'the raging one'. Name of one of the great heroines of Ireland.

Delia (g) Greek; a surname of the goddess Diana.

Delicia (g) Italian; 'delightful'.

Demetrius (b) Greek; 'working for Demeter'. Demeter was the protectress of the fruits of the earth.

Dennis, Denis (b) Greek; a contraction of Dionysos, the Greek God of wine. *Dim.* DENNY.

Denise (g) French feminine equivalent of the above.

Derek, Derrick (b) Teutonic; 'peoples' wealth'. *Dim.* DERRY, RICK.

Desmond (b) Celtic; originally a clan-name, meaning South Munster. *Dim.* DES, DESIE.

Diana (g) Latin; name of the Roman Goddess of Light, in Greek known as ARTEMIS. Popularised by English poets of the Restoration.

Diggory (b) Old French; etymology obscure, possibly means 'lost'. Now considered to be a rustic name.

Dinah (g) Hebrew; 'judged'. Not to be confused etymologically with DIANA.

Dolores (g) Spanish; 'grief'. Mainly a Roman Catholic name derived from Maria de Dolores, Our Lady of Sorrows.

Dominic (b) Latin; 'born on the Lord's day'. Popularised by the Dominicans, or the Black Friars.

Donald (b) Gaelic; 'ruler of the world'. Mainly Scottish. *Dim.* DON.

Dora (g) Originally a contraction of DOROTHEA, q.v. Associated with David Copperfield's wife and popular in late Victorian times.

Dorcas (g) Greek; 'gazelle'. A name now associated with charitable work.

Doreen (g) Celtic; 'sullen', or possibly a derivative of DORA.

Doris (g) Greek; meaning obscure, possibly 'of the sea'.

Dorothea, Dorothy (g) Greek; 'a gift of God'. *Dim.* DOLLY, DOT, DOTTY.

Douglas (b) Celtic; 'dark stream'. Almost solely Scottish. *Dim.* DOUG, DOUGGIE.

Drusilla (g) Latin; feminine diminutive of 'a strong man'. *Dim.* DRUSIE.

Dugald (b) Celtic; 'dark stranger'. Scottish. *Dim.* DUG, DUGGIE.

Dulcibella (g) 'sweet' or 'mild', originally Latin. Associated names are DULCINEA, DULCIA, DULCIE.

Duncan (b) Celtic; 'brown warrior'. Popular Scottish name.

Dunstan (b) Anglo-Saxon; 'hill-stone'. Popularised by the Dunstan who was an abbot of Glastonbury, and Archbishop of Canterbury in the 10th Century.

Dylan (b) Welsh; 'the sea'.

EDWINA

E

Eaditha (g) A variant of Edith, q.v.

Eamon (b) Irish form of Edmund, q.v.

Ebenezer (b) Hebrew; 'stone of help'. *Dim.* EB, EBBIE.

Edgar (b) Anglo-Saxon; 'fortunate spear'. Lack of popularity may be due to the illegitimate prince of that name in Shakespeare's "King Lear".

Edith (g) Anglo-Saxon; 'prosperous war'. *Dim.* EDIE.

Edmond, Edmund (b) Anglo-Saxon; 'happy protector'.

Edna (g) Hebrew or Celtic; origin obscure. Possibly the feminine form of Edwin.

Edward (b) Anglo-Saxon; 'rich guardian'. One of the earliest royal names. *Dim.* ED, EDDIE, TED, TEDDY.

Edwin (b) Anglo-Saxon; 'rich friend'.

Edwina (g) Feminine form of Edwin.

Egbert (b) Anglo-Saxon; 'formidably bright'.

Egmond, Egmont (b) Teutonic; 'terrible protection'.

Eileen (g) An Irish form of either Helen, or Evelyn, q.v. Sometimes spelt AILEEN.

Elaine (g) A variant of Helen, q.v. Gained popularity in Victorian times from Tennyson's Idyll "Lancelot and Elaine".

Eleanor, Eleanora (g) English variants of Helen, q.v.

Eli (b) Hebrew; 'exalted'. Also used as a contraction of ELIAS, ELIJAH.

Elias (b) Hebrew; 'God the Lord'.

Elijah (b) Hebrew; 'Jehovah is God'.

Elise, Eliza (g) Contraction of Elizabeth, q.v.

Elizabeth (g) Hebrew; 'oath of God'. Perhaps the most popular English girls' name, it is also found spelt with an 's'. *Dim.* BESSY, BETTY, LIZ, LIZZIE, LISA, LIBBY, BETH.

Ellen (g) Scottish variant of Helen; *Con.* ELLA.

Eloïse (g) Feminine derivatives of Louis; 'famous war'. Popularised from France by the story of "Héloïse and Abélard.

Elsie (g) Contraction of Elizabeth.

Elspeth (g) Scottish; contraction of Elizabeth.

Elvira (g) Old German; 'elf-counsel'.

Emerald, Esmerelda (g) One of the jewel names.

Emil, Emile (b) Old French; 'industrious'.

Emily, Emilie, Emilia, Amelia (g) Feminine equivalents of the above. *Dim.* EMMIE, EM, EMMELINE, EMMELINA.

Emlyn (b) Welsh form of the now extinct ERMIN; 'work serpent'.

Emma (g) Teutonic; contraction of ERMENTRUDE. No association with EMILY and its derivatives, or with EMMANUEL.

Emmanuel (b) Hebrew; 'God with us'. Uncommon except with Roman Catholics, and those of Italian extraction. There is also a feminine form, EMMANUELA, which is almost unknown in England.

Ena (g) Either Greek 'praise'; feminine form of AENEAS; or the name-ending -ENA, used as a diminutive.

Enid (g) Celtic; 'spotless purity'.

Enoch (b) Hebrew; 'dedicated'. Closely associated nowadays with Tennyson's "Enoch Arden".

Ephraim (b) Hebrew; 'doubly fruitful'. Now more popular in America. *Dim.* EPH.

Erasmus (b) Greek; 'loved'. Introduced to England by the great Dutch scholar who assumed the name.

Eric (b) Norse; 'ever king'. Now only just recovering from the effects of the publication of "Eric, or Little by Little", by Dean Farrar.

Erica (g) Feminine form of the above.

Ermentrude (g) Teutonic; 'maid of the nation'.

Ernest (b) Teutonic; 'grave, serious'. *Dim.* ERN, ERNIE.

Errol (b) Latin; 'wanderer'.

Esau (b) Hebrew; 'hairy'.

Esmê (b and g) French; 'esteemed'.

Esmond (b) Teutonic; 'divine protection'.

Estelle, Estella (g) Diminutive of ESTHER, with STELLA; 'a star'.

Esther (g) Persian; 'star'. Also found as HESTER.

Ethel (g) Anglo-Saxon; 'noble'. Originally found almost entirely as a prefix, but now stands alone.

Eugene (b) Greek; 'well-born'. *Dim.* GENE, GENIE.

Eugenia, Eugenie (g) Feminine form of the above.

Eunice (g) Greek; 'happy victory'; 'wife'.

Euphemia (g) Greek; 'fair speech'. *Dim.* EFFIE, EPHIE.

Eustace (b) Greek; 'happy harvest'. For some reason now considered a ridiculous name, probably because of its association with 'useless' e.g., 'useless Eustace'.

Eva, Eve (g) Translation of the Greek ZOE; 'life'.

Evadne (g) Greek; 'well-tamed'. In the play of Aeschylus she leaps into the flames that burn her husband's body.

Evan (b) Celtic; 'young warrior', and also a Welsh form of JOHN. Also found as EWEN and EWAN.

Evangelinė (g) Greek; 'happy messenger'.

Evelyn (b and g) Celtic; 'pleasant'. Other forms are EVELEEN, EVELINE, EVELINA (popularised by Fanny Burney), all of which are feminine. *Dim.* EVIE, EVVIE.

Everard (b) Teutonic; 'brave as a boar'. *Con.* EWART, one of Mr. Gladstone's names.

Ezekiel (b) Hebrew; 'God will strengthen'.

Ezra (b) Hebrew; 'help'. More popular in America than in England, and name of the American poet Ezra Pound.

F

FRIEDA

Fabian (b) Latin; 'bean-grower'. Now connected with left-wing politics.

Faith (g) One of the abstract quality names, invariably associated with HOPE and CHARITY. *Con.* FAY, evolved from the French *foi*.

fraser

Fanny (g) A contraction of Frances, q.v., but often used independently.

Felicity (g) Latin; 'happiness'. FELICIA is also found.

Felix (b) Latin; 'happy'. Strangely associated with cats.

Ferdinand (b) Teutonic; 'venturous life'. *Dim.* FERDIE.

Fergus (b) Celtic; 'man's strength'. *Dim.* FERGIE.

Finella, Fenella (g) Celtic; 'white-shouldered'. From the Celtic FINN or FIONN, the Irish legendary hero.

Fingal (b) Celtic; 'fair stranger'.

Fiona (g) Celtic; 'white girl'.

Flavia (g) Latin; 'golden'.

Flavian (b) Masculine form of the above.

Fleur (g) French; 'flower'.

Flora (g) Latin; 'flower'.

Florence (g) Latin; 'blooming'. *Dim.* FLO, FLORRIE, FLOSSIE.

(b) Celtic; 'fair offspring'. Found almost solely in Ireland.

Frances (g) **Francis** (b) Old German; 'free'. The widespread use of this name derives in part from the popular St. Francis. *Dim.* (b) FRANCIS: FRANK, FRANKIE; *Dim.* (g) FRANCES: FRAN, FRANCIE, FANNY, FAN.

Franklin (g) Teutonic; 'freeholder'. Diminutives same as above. Owes its popularity in America to Benjamin Franklin and to Franklin D. Roosevelt, the famous war-time President.

Freda (g) Contraction of Winifred, q.v.

Frederick, Frederic (b) Old German; 'peaceful ruler' *Con.* FREDRIC. *Dim.* FREDDIE, FRED.

Frederica (g) Feminine variant of the above. *Dim.* FREDDIE.

Frida, Frieda (g) German; 'peace'. *Dim.* FREE.

Fulbert (b) Teutonic; 'exceeding bright'.

Fulk, Fulke (b) German; 'folk, people'.

19

G

GEORGE

Gabriel (b) Hebrew; 'man of God'. *Dim.* GABE.

Gabrielle, Gabriella (g) Feminine form of the above. *Dim.* GABIE.

Gareth (b) Anglo-Saxon; 'firm spear'. *Con.* GARTH. *Dim.* GARRY, GARRIE.

Gavin (b) Celtic; 'hawk of the month of May'. Contraction of the following.

Gawain, Gawaine (b) Appears in Tennyson's "Idylls of the King".

Gay (g). Derives directly from the adjective "*gay*".

Gemma (g) Italian; 'precious stone'.

Genevieve (g) Latin; 'fair girl'.

Genevra (g) Contraction of GUINEVERE q.v.

Geoffrey (b) Teutonic; 'God's peace'. Also found spelt JEFFREY, GEOFFROY. *Dim.* GEOFF, JEFF. One of the oldest English names, and was borne by Chaucer.

George (b) Greek; 'husbandman, farmer'. Perhaps the most popular of the English boys' names, both of royalty and commoner, and also the name of the Patron saint of England. *Dim.* GEORGIE, GEORDIE.

Georgina, Georgiana (b) Feminine derivatives of the above. *Dim.* GEORGIE, GINA.

Gerald (b) Teutonic; 'firm spear'. *Dim.* GERRIE, GERRY.

Geraldine (g) Feminine form of the above. *Dim.* GERRIE, GERRY.

Gerard (b) English contraction of Gerald.

Gertrude (g) Teutonic; 'spear maiden'. *Dim.* GERT, GERTIE, GATTY.

Gervase, Gervaise (b) Teutonic; 'spear-eagerness'. Also found as JERVIS, JARVIS.

Gideon (b) Hebrew; 'feller of men'.

Gilbert (b) Old German; 'bright pledge'. *Dim.* GIL, GILLIE, BERT.

Gilchrist (b) Celtic; 'servant of Christ'.

Giles (b) Greek; origin obscure. St. Giles was the patron saint of cripples and beggars.

Gillian (g) Popular English form of JULIA, q.v.

Gisela (g) Feminine form of Gilbert, q.v.

Githa (g) Anglo-Saxon; meaning obscure. Possibly contraction of Eaditha, or means 'gift'.

Gwladys (g) Welsh form of CLAUDIA; 'lame'. *Dim.* GLAD.

Gloria (g) Latin; 'fame'. A modern Christian name. Possibly influenced by Gloriana, one of the names of Queen Elizabeth. *Dim.* GOR.

Goddard (b) German; 'strong in God'.

Godfrey (b) Teutonic; 'God's peace'. Another form of GEOFFREY.

Gordon (b) Scottish; 'from the three-cornered hill'. Popularity greatly increased due to the fame of General Gordon.

Grace (g) Latin; 'thanks'. One of the abstract virtue names. Very popular in Ireland where it has been used for GRANIA, one of the legendary heroines of that country. *Dim.* GRACIE.

Graham, Grahame (b) Celtic; 'from the grey house'. Mainly Scottish.

Gregory (b) Greek; 'watchman'. A name found frequently among early Christians. *Dim.* GREG, GRIG.

Greta (g) Norse; contraction of the old Norse GRETTA, itself a contraction of MARGARET, q.v.

Griseldis, Griselda (g) Teutonic; 'grey battle-maid'. Associated with Boccaccio's tale of the perfect patient wife. *Dim.* GRIZ, GRIZZEL, GRIZZIE, GIRZIE, GRITTY.

Guinevere (g) Celtic; 'white wave'. Name of the wife of King Arthur. *Con.* GINEVRA. *Dim.* GWINNY.

Gustavus (b) Teutonic; 'divine staff'. GUSTAVE is also found.

• **Guy** (b) Old German; 'leader'. The feminine form GUIDA is less commonly found.

Gwendolen, Gwendoline, (g) Celtic; 'white-browed'. *Dim.* GWEN, GWYNNE, GWENNIE.

Gwyneth (g) Welsh; 'blessed'. Equivalent of Beatrice. *Dim.* GWYN.

H

HARRIET

Hagar (g) Hebrew; 'forsaken'.

Haggai (g) Hebrew; 'festival of the Lord'. Name of a minor prophet.

Halbert (b) Teutonic; 'bright stone'.

Hallam (b) Formerly a surname, and used as a Christian name only since 1833 when Arthur Hallam, friend of Lord Tennyson died and was immortalised in "In Memoriam", perhaps the finest commemorative poem in the English language.

Hamo (b) Teutonic; 'home'. Sometimes spelt 'HAYMO'. *Dim.* HAMLYN.

Hannah (g) Hebrew; early version of Anne, q.v.

Hannibal (b) Phoenician; 'grace of Baal'. Popular in Cornwall.

Hanno (b) Phoenician; 'grace'. Another Cornish name.

Harold, Harald (b) Norse; 'great general'.

Harriet (g) Teutonic; 'home-rule'. Feminine version of HARRY, itself often a contraction of HENRY.

Harry (b) Contraction of HENRY, q.v. and often used independently.

Hartley (b) Anglo-Saxon; 'stony meadow'. Now mainly a surname.

Harvey (b) Celtic; 'bitter', derived from the French 'HERVE', 'warrior'.

Hazel (g) Teutonic; from the tree so called.

Heather (g) From the flower.

Hebe (g) Greek goddess of youth who waited on the gods. Now unfortunately connected with barmaids.

Hector (b) Greek; 'defender'. Name of the Trojan hero who fought with, and was killed by, Achilles. *Dim.* HEC.

Helen, Helena (g) Greek; 'light', Name of the beautiful wife of Menelaus, whose 'face launched a thousand ships'. The source of many names: ELLEN EILEEN, ELEANOR, etc.

Henrietta (g) The feminine form of HENRY. *Dim* HATTY, HETTY, HITTY, ETTY, ETTA.

Henry (b) Old German; 'home-rule'. *Con.* HARRY. A popular royal name in England, and in foreign versions in France and Germany also.

Hepzibah (g) Hebrew; 'my delight is in her'. *Dim.* HEP.

Herbert (b) Teutonic; 'bright army'. As well as a Christian name one of the oldest surnames in England. *Dim.* HERB, HERBIE, BERT.

Hercules (b) Greek; 'lordly fame'. Associated uniquely

with the classical Strong Man, and his seven labours.

Hermia (g) Greek; either the feminine of HERMES, or a contraction of HERMIONE.

Hermione (g) Greek; 'daughter of Hermes'.

Hero (g) Greek; 'mistress of the house'. Hero and Leander were two of the world's greatest lovers.

Hew, Hu (b) Welsh variant of Hugh, q.v.

Hezekiah (g) Hebrew; 'strength of the Lord'.

Hilary (b and g) Latin; 'cheerful'.

Hilda (g) Teutonic; 'battle-maid' Name of the chief of the Valkyries.

Hildebrand (b) Teutonic; 'battle-sword'.

Hildegarde (g) Teutonic; 'battle-maid'.

Hippolytus (b) Greek; 'freer of horses'. A classical and pastoral name. The feminine HIPPOLYTA is occasionally found.

Hiram (b) Hebrew, from the same root as JEROME, q.v. Now found almost entirely in America.

Hobart (b) Variant of HUBERT, q.v.

Homer (b) Greek; 'pledge'. Name of the great Greek poet.

Honor, Honoria (g) Latin; 'honour'.

Hope (g) One of the abstract virtue names; it is some times given to boys.

Horace, Horatio (b) Latin; 'punctual'. Interest in this name has been kept alive by its illustrious bearers; the Roman poet, Horace Walpole, and Lord Nelson, to name but three.

Horatia (g) Feminine version of the above.

Hortensia, Hortense (g) Latin; 'gardener'.

Howard (b) Old French; either 'an osprey' or 'sword-guardian'. Originally one of the oldest surnames in England, it is now frequently used as a Christian name.

Hubert (b) Teutonic; 'bright of mind'. St. Hubert was the patron saint of hunters. *Dim.* BERT.

Hugh (b) Teutonic; 'mind, spirit'. *Dim.* HUGHIE.

Hugo (b) Originally the Latin version of the above, but now occasionally used independently.

Humfrey, Humphrey (b) Teutonic; 'giant peace'. *Dim.* HUM. HUMP, HUMPIE, HUMPS, NUMPS.

Hyacinth (g) Greek; 'purple'. Found mainly among the Irish where its popularity is due to various saints of that name. *Dim.* HY, SINTY.

IGNATIUS

Ian, Iain (b) Scottish form of JOHN, q.v.

Ianthe (g) Greek; 'violet flower'.

Ida (g) Teutonic; 'labour', or sometimes Celtic; 'thirsty'. There is no connection with Mount Ida.

Ifor (b) Welsh form of IVOR, q.v.

Ignatius (b) Latin; 'fiery'. A popular name among Roman Catholics.

Imogen, Imogine (g) Anglo-Saxon; 'daughter', or sometimes supposed to mean 'last-born'.

Ines, Inez (g) Spanish form of the Latin 'Agnus', 'lamb', and therefore the same as AGNES.

Ingram (b) Teutonic; 'Ing's raven'. Ing was a legendary Scandinavian hero.

Ingrid (g) Norwegian; 'Ing's ride'. The popularity of this name in England is recent and is probably due to a Hollywood star's name.

Inigo (b) Contraction of IGNATIUS, q.v. Name of the well-known early seventeenth century architect and carver, Inigo Jones.

Innocent (b) Latin ; 'harmless, innocent'. Rare except

25

among Roman Catholics, it has been the name of thirteen popes.

Iolanthe (g) Origin and meaning obscure. The name has been kept alive by the Gilbert and Sullivan opera in this country, and is found in America as YOLANDE *Dim*. Io.

Ira (g) Hebrew; 'watchful'.

Irene (g) Greek; 'messenger of peace'. Properly, this name should have three syllables. *Dim*. RENIE.

Iris (g) Greek; 'rainbow', but it is often used as a flower name.

Isa (g) German; 'iron'.

Isaac (b) Hebrew; 'laughter'. Also spelt IZAAK. Borne by the author of *The Compleat Angler*, Izaak Walton. *Dim*. IKE. Now usually a Jewish name.

Isabel, Isobel (g) Variant of Elizabeth, and more common in Scotland and France. Another form, ISABELLA is mainly Spanish in use. *Con*. ISBEL, ISHBEL. *Dim*. ISA, BELLE.

Isadora (g) Feminine of ISIDOR, q.v. Name of the interpretative dancer, Isadora Duncan, who died in 1927.

Ishmael (b) Hebrew; 'God hearkens'.

Isidor, Isidore (b) Greek; 'gift of Isis'. *Dim*. IZZY.

Isold, Isolde, Isolda, Iseult, Ysolt (g) Celtic; 'spectacle'. Tristram and Isolde were two legendary Celtic lovers, and the subject of a Wagnerian opera.

Ivan (b) Russian form of John, q.v. Rare in England since the Russian revolution of 1917.

Ivo (b) Celtic form of JOHN, q.v. from the Breton 'Yves'. Rare in England now, but there was a St. Ivo who gave his name to the St. Ives in Cornwall, and in Huntingdonshire.

Ivor (b) Norse; 'protector of Ing'. Its use is mainly restricted to those of Celtic extraction.

Ivy (g) Teutonic; 'clinging'. One of the plant names, like HAZEL.

J

JULIA

Jabez (b) Hebrew; 'causing pain'. More common in America than in England. *Dim.* JABE.

Jacintha (g) Variant of HYACINTH, q.v. *Dim.* JACKIE.

Jack (b) Originally a diminutive of JOHN, it is now used independently. It is also used generically for men, e.g. "every man-jack", "Jack Frost", "Jack Tar", etc. *Dim.* Jacky.

Jacob (b) Hebrew; 'the supplanter'. *Dim.* JAKE.

Jacobina (g) Scottish feminine version of the above.

Jacqueline (g) French feminine version of JAQUES (JAMES). *Dim.* JACKIE.

James (b) Hebrew; derived from Ja'akob, 'a heel', because Jacob took his brother Esau by the heel in the womb. The French form, JAQUES, is occasionally found as a Christian name in England. The Irish version (SEAMUS) and the Scottish version (HAMISH) are also found. James has been a favourite royal name. *Dim.* JAMIE, JIM.

Jamesina (g) Scottish feminine version of the above.

Jan (b) Welsh form of JOHN, q.v.

Jane (g) Contraction of JOANNA, q.v. *Dim.* JANIE.

Janet, Jannet, Janette (g) Originally diminutives of JANE.

Janice (g) Hebrew: 'Gift of God'.

Jasmine (g) Flower name, originally Persian. Increased popularity was due to James Elroy Flecker's 'Hassan'. *Dim*. JESS, JASSY.

Jasper (b) Persian; 'master of the treasure'. The variant CASPAR, or KASPAR, is sometimes found.

Jean (g) Originally a Scottish variant of JANE and JOAN, it is now widely used independently and is one of the most popular girl's names.

Jefferson (b) Originally a surname, it is now sometimes used as a Christian name, particularly in America where its popularity is owed to the third President. *Dim*. JEFF.

Jemima (g) Hebrew; 'handsome as the day', or Arabic; 'a dove'. *Dim*. JEMMA, MIMA.

Jennifer (g) A variant of GUINEVERE, q.v. Also found spelt JENNEFER, JENEFER. *Dim*. JENNY, JEN.

Jenny Besides being a diminutive of JENNIFER, and JANE, this is sometimes bestowed independently.

Jeremiah (b) Hebrew; 'appointed by God'. *Dim*. JERRY.

Jeremy (b) Contraction of the above and more frequently used in England. *Dim*. JERRY.

Jerome, Jerram (b) Greek; 'holy name'. The old form HIERONYMO was still found occasionally in Shakespearean England. The name is associated with St. Jerome and the lions. *Dim*. JERRY.

Jesse (b) Hebrew; 'the true God'.

Jessica (g) Hebrew; 'God is looking'. Introduced to England in Shakespeare's "Merchant of Venice". *Dim*. JESS, JESSIE.

Jessie (g) As well as being a diminutive of the above, this name is sometimes given independently.

Jill (g) A contraction of GILLIAN, q.v. Also used generically for women, as the feminine equivalent of JACK.

Joachim (b) Hebrew; 'appointed of the Lord'.

Joan (g) Contraction of JOANNA, but now more frequent and used independently.

Joanna, Johanna (g) Hebrew; 'grace of the Lord'. *Dim.* Jo. The source of ANNE, JOAN, JEAN, JANE, etc. and their derivatives.

Job (b) Hebrew; 'persecuted'. Associated with enduring patience.

Jocelin, Jocelyn (b) Origin obscure. Either Teutonic, or derived from the Breton St. Josse.

Joceline (g) Feminine form of the above.

Jock (b) Scottish diminutive for JOHN, and also used generically for Scotsmen.

Joel (b) Hebrew; 'Jehovah is God'.

John (b) From the same root as JOHANNA, JOHN is found in various forms in all countries of Europe and the Middle East, and is the most popular boys' name. The variants and diminutives are innumerable. This popularity is due mainly to St. John the Evangelist, and St. John the Baptist, each of whom have two feast days in the Roman Catholic Church. There are over eighty Sts. John. *Dim.* JACK, JOHNNY, JOHNNIE. Also found spelt JON.

Jolyon (b) May be a derivative of JOHN, or from the French '*joli*'. Introduced by Galsworthy's "Forsyte Saga".

Jonah (b) Hebrew; 'a dove'. As a result of the original Jonah being swallowed by a fish the name has come to be used of any bearer of bad-luck.

Jonas (b) A Greek and Latin form of the above.

Jonathan (b) Hebrew; 'the Lord's gift'. Associated with the friendship of David and Jonathan.

Jordan (b) Hebrew; 'descender'. The custom of baptism in the river Jordan probably gave rise to the use of this name, which is now rare.

Joseph (m) Hebrew; 'he shall add'. *Dim.* JOE. The Latin form JOSEPHUS is also occasionally found.

Josepha (g) The feminine form of JOSEPHUS.

29

Josephine (g) A feminine diminutive of Joseph. Inclined to be associated with Napoleon's wife. *Dim.* Jo, Jose, Pheeny.

Joshua (b) Hebrew; 'Jehovah is salvation'. *Dim.* Josh, Jos.

Josiah (b) Hebrew; 'Jehovah supports'. Name of the first famous member of the Wedgewood family.

Joy (g) One of the abstract virtue names.

Joyce (g) Celtic; from the name of the Breton St. Josse. Originally used for both sexes.

Juanita (g) Spanish form of JOHANNA, q.v. *Dim.* Nita.

Jude, Judas (b) Hebrew; 'praise of the Lord'. The latter is unpopular because of the connection with Judas Iscariot. The former is associated with St. Jude, and Hardy's "Jude the Obscure".

Judith, Judy (g) Hebrew; 'a jewess'. The latter was originally a diminutive of the former, but now usually used independently.

Julia (g) Latin; feminine form of JULIUS, but now more common. *Dim.* Julie, which is also sometimes used independently.

Julian (b) Latin; a derivative of JULIUS, q.v.

Juliana (g) Feminine version of the above, and also the source of GILLIAN, JILL, etc.

Juliet, Juliette (g) Originally a diminutive of JULIA, it is now always used independently and owes its popularity to Shakespeare's play "Romeo and Juliet". *Dim.* Julie.

Julius (b) Originally Greek; 'first growth of beard' i.e. 'youthful', but more often associated with Julius Caesar, the most famous of a well-known Roman family.

June (g) Name of the month, as APRIL.

Justin (b) Latin; diminutive of JUSTUS (also occasionally found) 'JUST'. Name of the second century Christian martyr.

Justina (g) Latin; feminine version of the above.

K

Karen (g) Danish; 'pure'. *Dim.* KAY.

Katherine, Kathleen, etc. (g) See CATHERINE.

Kay (g) Diminutive of KAREN, and also of KATHERINE, but sometimes used independently.

Kean (b) Celtic; 'vast'.

Keith (b) Gaelic; 'wind'.

Kenelm (b) Anglo-Saxon; 'bold helmet'.

Kenneth (b) Celtic; 'handsome'. *Dim.* KEN, KENNY.

Kevin (b) Irish version of KENNETH and name of one of the patron saints of Dublin.

Keziah (b) Hebrew; one of the three beautiful daughters of Job.

Kieron, Kieren (b) Celtic; 'swarthy'. Name of another Irish saint.

Kirstin, Kirsten (g) Scottish and Norse contraction of Christian. *Dim.* KIRSTY, KRISTY.

LLEW

L

Laghlan (b) Celtic; 'warlike'. Found only in Scotland and Ireland.

Lalage (g) Greek; 'prattler'.

Lambert (b) Old German; 'pride of the land'. Now more usual as a surname.

Lalita (g) Sanskrit; 'artless'.

Lana (g) Greek; 'light'. Popularised by a Hollywood film star.

31

Lancelot, Launcelot (b) Latin; 'boy-servant'. Famous hero of Arthurian romantic legend thus named led to its being associated with chivalry. *Dim.* LANCE.

Laura (g) Latin; 'laurel tree'. Heroine of Petrarchian sonnets. *Dim.* LOLLY, LAURETTA.

Laurence, Lawrence (b) Greek; 'laurel tree'. *Dim.* LARRY, LANTY, LAURIE.

Larkin (b) English contraction of the above.

Lavinia (g) Latin; 'a woman from Lavinium'. *Dim.* VINNY.

Lazarus (b) Latin; 'whom God assists'. Name of the mediaeval beggar who was the patron saint of lepers.

Leander (b) Greek; 'lion-man'. Leander was the famous lover who swam the Hellespont every night to visit Hero. Now the name is associated with the rowing club of the same name.

Leigh, Lee (b and g) Anglo-Saxon; 'meadow'. Now rare.

Leila (g) Arabic; 'darkness'. Perhaps a contraction of Delilah.

Lemuel (b) Hebrew; 'devoted to God'. Christian name of Swift's Gulliver, and of a hero in American detective fiction. *Dim.* LEMMY.

Lena (g) Contraction of ELEANORA, and LEONORA, but sometimes used independently.

Leo (b) Greek; 'lion'. Fifth sign of the Zodiac.

Leonie (g) French feminine version of the above.

Leonard (b) Teutonic; 'lion-strong'. *Dim.* LEN, LENNIE.

Leopold (b) Old German; 'people-bold'.

Lesbia (g) Latin; 'girl from Lesbos'. A popular name among the Latin poets, but now more popular in Ireland.

Leslie (b and g) Origin obscure. Taken from the surname. *Dim.* LES.

Letitia (g) Latin; 'gladness'. *Dim.* LETTY.

Lettice (g) English contraction of the above.

Lewis (b) Celtic; 'lion-like' from LLEWELLYN, or French; 'famous', from LOUIS. CLOVIS is an obsolete version of the same name.

Liam (b) Irish version of WILLIAM, q.v.

Lida (g) Slavonic; 'people's love'.

Lilian, Lily, Lilias (g) Origin obscure. Either flower-names, or early contractions of ELIZABETH.

Linda (g) Originally contraction of MELINDA, BELINDA, etc., now often independently bestowed.

Lionel (b) Greek; 'little lion'.

Llew (b) Welsh; 'lion'.

Llewellyn (b) Celtic; 'lion-like'.

Lloyd (b) Celtic; 'grey'.

Lodowick, Ludovic (b) Teutonic; 'famous'. *Dim* LUDO.

Lois (g) Originally a contraction of ALOISIA; 'famous war', it is now more common than its root.

Lola (g) Diminutive of DOLORES, q.v.

Lorna, Lorne (g) Anglo-Saxon; 'love-lorn, lost'. Owes it popularity to the novel "Lorna Doone."

Lothair, Lothario (b) French and Italian variants of the same root as LUDOVICK and LEWIS; 'famous'.

Louis (b) French version of LEWIS, q.v.

Louise, Louisa, Louie (g) Feminine versions of the above.

Loveday (b and g) Originally a Cornish surname, 'day appointed for reconciliations'.

Lubin (b) Teutonic; 'dear friend'.

Lucasta (g) Invented by the poet Lovelace and may refer to a member of the LUCAS family.

Lucian, Lucius (b) Latin; 'born in daylight'.

Lucretia (g) Latin; 'bringer of light'. Sometimes spelt LUCREZIA, as in the case of the infamous member of the Borgia family.

Lucy, Lucia (g) Feminine versions of LUCIUS, q.v. *Dim*. LUCILLA, LUCILIA, LUCINA, LUCETTA, LUCINDA.

Luke (b) Greek; 'coming from Lucania'. Associated

with the third Evangelist, 'Luke the Physician'. Sometimes found as LUCAS, though this is now mainly a surname.

Luther (b) Variant of LOTHAIR, q.v., made known by the German religious leader Martin Luther.

Lydia (g) Greek; 'a woman of Lydia'. The name became popular in England through the seventeenth century poets.

Lynn, Lynne (g) Anglo-Saxon; 'a cascade'.

M

MIRANDA

Mabel (g) Contraction of AMABEL, q.v. *Dim.* MAB, which in Ireland has become MAEVE, the name of one of the Irish legendary heroines.

Macaire (b) Greek; 'blessed', but found only in Ireland.

Mac (b) Diminutive of all names beginning with MAC, but very occasionally found independently.

Madeline, Madeleine (g) Contraction of MAG-DELEN, q.v. *Dim.* MADDY.

Madoc (b) Welsh; 'fortunate'.

Magdalen, Magdalene (g) Hebrew; 'woman of Magdala', Magdala being the birthplace of Mary Magdalene. *Dim.* MAGDA, which is sometimes used independently. MAGDALENA is also occasionally found.

Magnus (b) Latin; 'great'. Once a very popular name but now rare.

Maisie, Mysie (g) Originally Scottish diminutives of

MARGARET, but now always used independently.

Malachi (b) Hebrew; 'God's messenger'.

Malcolm (b) Celtic; 'servant of Colomba'. Found only in Scotland.

Malvina, Malvine (g) An invention by Macpherson in his Ossianic poems. Found in Scotland.

Mamie (g) Diminutive of MARGARET, q.v. now used independently especially in America.

Manoc (b) Hebrew; 'great'.

Manasseh (b) Hebrew; 'he who causes forgetfulness'.

Manfred (b) Old German; 'man of peace'. The name is kept alive by Byron's poem of that name.

Manuel (b) Contraction of EMMANUEL, q.v. *Dim.* MANNY.

Manus (b) Contraction of MAGNUS, q.v.

Marcella, Marcelia (g) Latin; contraction of MARCELLUS, q.v.

Marcellus (b) Latin; diminutive of MARCUS, q.v.

Marcia (g) Feminine of MARCUS, q.v.

Marcius, Marco (b) Latin and Italian forms of MARCUS, q.v.

Marcus (b) Latin; name of the God of War.

Margaret (g) Greek; 'a pearl', from the Persian 'child of light' because the Persians thought the pearls rose to the surface of the water at night to worship the moon and were in fact made by the congealing of the dew by the moonlight. *Dim.* MAGGIE, MADGE, MEG, MEGGY, MARGET, PEGGY, GRETA, MAISIE.

Margareta, Margarita, Marguerita (g) German, Spanish and French forms of the above. *Dim.* GRETA, MARGA, RITA.

Margot (g) French contraction of MARGUERITE, but used independently. Name of the famous English ballerina, and of Lady Oxford, famed for her wit.

Maria (g) An early form of MARY, q.v., but now less popular in England.

Marian, Marion (g) An early diminutive of MARY, q.v., very popular in the Middle Ages, and borne by Maid Marion, Robin Hood's lady.

Mariana (g) A Spanish form of MARIA. The name bears the stigma of Tennyson's poems about a Mariana who was 'a-weary, a-weary'.

Marianne (g) A French contraction of MARIE-ANNE.

Marie (g) French form of MARIA, but sometimes used in England either independently or, as in France, with another name, e.g. MARIE-LOUISE.

Mariette (g) French diminutive of the above.

Marigold (g) One of the flower names. *Dim.* MALLY.

Marina (g) Latin; 'of the sea'. This name has become popular in England following the marriage in 1934 of Princess Marina of Greece with the late Duke of Kent.

Marius (b) Latin; 'of Mars'. Made popular in England by Walter Pater's "Marius the Epicurean".

Marjorie, Marjery (g) A Scottish variant of MARGARET, q.v. *Dim.* MARGE, MARGIE.

Mark (b) Originally probably from the same root as MARCUS, but owes its popularity mainly to St. Mark, and also slightly to Mark Anthony.

Marmaduke (b) Celtic; 'sea leader'. *Con.* DUKE, which is sometimes given independently.

Mario (b) Hebrew; 'bitterness'. A masculine form of MARIA.

Martha, Marta (g) Aramaic; 'a lady'. From the Bible it derives its association with humility, low-birth. *Dim.* MARTITA, MARTIE.

Martin (b) Latin; diminutive of MARTIUS; 'belonging to Mars'. There are two Sts. Martin, the better-known of whom is the patron saint of inn-keepers and is usually portrayed sharing his cloak with a beggar.

Martina (g) Feminine version of MARTIN.

Mary (g) The English form of MARIA, which is

derived from MIRIAM—Hebrew; 'bitterness'. In the Middle Ages there was a movement to derive Mary from 'of the sea'. The name came to England from France and it was not until the time of Mary II that the name was spelt as it is today. It is perhaps the most usual girls' name and this popularity is partly due to royal patronage and largely also to Roman Catholic influence, after the Virgin Mary, and Mary Magdalene. *Dim.* MOL, MOLLY, POL, POLLY.

Marylyn (g) Probably a diminutive of MARY. *Con.* MARLENE and MAUREEN.

Matilda (g) Teutonic; 'mighty battle-maid'. Now associated with Belloc's Matilda who 'told such dreadful lies'. *Dim.* MATTY, TILLY.

Matthew (b) Hebrew; 'gift of the Lord'. This name is far less popular than those of the other Evangelists. *Dim.* MATT.

Matthias (b) Variant of the above.

Maud, Maude (g) From the same route as MATILDA, q.v. Now associated with Tennyson's "Come into the Garden, Maud". *Dim.* MAUDIE.

Maudlin, Maun (g) English contraction of MAG-DALENE, q.v.

Maureen (g) Irish contraction of MARY, through MARYLYN.

Mavis (g) Old English name for a song-thrush. First introduced by Marie Corelli in one of her novels.

Maximilian, Maxim (b) Latin; 'greatest'. Formerly a favourite name with Middle European royalty. *Dim.* MAX, MAXIE.

May (g) Contraction of MARY and MARGARET, but often given independently of either. The spelling MAE has been popularised by Hollywood.

Maynard (b) Old German; 'firmness'. Borne by the late well-known economist and patron of the arts, Lord Keynes.

Mehitabel, Mehetobel (g) Hebrew; 'beneficient'.

Melanie (g) Greek; 'dark-complexioned'. *Dim*. MELLY.

Melchior (b) Hebrew; 'God is light'.

Melina, Melinda (g) Origin obscure. Perhaps Greek; 'of the ash-tree'.

Melissa (g) Greek; 'honey'. *Dim*. LISSA

Melitta (g) A variant of the above.

Melody (g) An old English abstract name.

Malva (g) Celtic; 'chief'.

Mercedes (g) Spanish; from MARIA DE LAS MERCEDES, 'Mary of the Mercies'.

Mercia (g) Anglo-Saxon; 'woman from the border lands'.

Mercy (g) One of the abstract virtue names, but less popular than most of them.

Meredith (b and g) Welsh; 'sea-protector'. *Dim*. MERRY.

Merle (g) French; 'blackbird'. Popularised by Hollywood.

Merlin (b) Welsh; 'sea-hill'. The name is associated with magicians.

Mervin, Mervyn, Marvyn (b) Anglo-Saxon; 'famous friend'. *Dim*. MAR, MER, MERV.

Meyrick (b) Teutonic; 'work-ruler'.

Micah (b) Hebrew; contraction of Michael, but used apart.

Michael (b) Hebrew; 'like to God'. One of the most popular boys' names in England, perhaps originally due to the Archangel Michael. *Dim*. MIKE, MICK, MICKY. All the diminutives are very popular in Ireland.

Mildred (g) Teutonic; 'mild power'. *Dim*. MILLY. The form MILDREDA is occasionally found.

Miles, Myles (b) Origin obscure. Perhaps Slavonic; 'merciful', or Greek; 'millstone'. Frequently found in Ireland.

Milicent, Millicent, Mellicent (g) Teutonic; 'work-strong'. *Dim*. MILLY.

Melisande, Melusine (g) French variants of the above.

Minerva (g) Greek goddess of learning.

Minnie, Minna (g) Teutonic; 'love'. MINA and MINELLA are also found as diminutives of this as well as of WILHELMINA, q.v.

Mirabel, Mirabella (g) Latin; 'wonderful'.

Miranda (g) Latin; 'worthy of admiration'. Kept alive by character of that name in Shakespeare's "Tempest".

Miriam (g) Earliest form of MARY, q.v.

Moira (g) Celtic; 'soft'. Sometimes found as MAURA. Usually found only in Ireland.

Mona (g) Greek; 'unique'. Associated with the famous portrait "Mona Lisa" by Leonardo da Vinci.

Monica (g) Origin obscure; but possibly Greek; 'unique'.

Montague, Montagu (b) French; 'peaked hill'. Now usually a surname. *Dim.* MONTY.

Morgan (b) Welsh; 'sea-dweller'. Also frequently found as a surname.

Morna (g) Gaelic; 'beloved'.

Morrice, Morris, Maurice (b) Greek; 'dark'. Frequently a surname.

Mortimer (b) Celtic; 'sea-warrior'. *Dim.* MORT MORTIE.

Moses (b) Either Coptic; 'saved from the water', or Hebrew; 'law-giver'. Usually now a Jewish name, and also often a surname. *Dim.* MOSE, Mo.

Mungo (b) Celtic; 'lovable'.

Muriel (g) Celtic; 'sea-white'. The form MERIEL is also found.

Murphy (b) Celtic; 'sea man'. Now usually an Irish surname.

Murdock, Murtagh (b) Celtic; 'sea-warrior'. Also often a surname.

Myfanwy (g) Celtic; either 'child of the water', or 'my fine one'. Used mostly in Wales.

Myra, Mira (g) Contraction of MIRANDA. Name of the well-known pianist, Dame Myra Hess.

Myrtle (g) Greek; the name of the shrub, which is sacred to Venus.

Mysie (g) Scottish contraction of MARGARET.

N

NITA

Nadine (g) Russian; 'hope'.

Nancy (g) Originally a variant of ANNE or AGNES, but now independently given. *Dim.* NAN, NANCE.

Naomi (g) Hebrew; 'my fine one'.

Napoleon (b) Italian; 'belonging to a new city'. An accepted name, but not in England, long before Napoleon Bonaparte.

Narcissus (b) Greek; 'daffodil'. Now rare, but used to be given as a flower-name and not in reference to the youth of Greek mythology.

Natalie (g) Latin; 'birth' (of Christ).

Nathaniel (b) Hebrew; 'gift of God'. *Con.* NATHAN. *Dim.* NAT, NATTY.

Neal, Neil, Neill, Nial (b) Celtic; 'champion'.

Nell, Nelly, Nellie (g) Originally diminutives of HELEN, these names are sometimes given independently.

Nelson (b) Name of the great British sailor, and dates entirely from his victories at sea.

Nesta, Nessie (g) Originally Scottish diminutives of

AGNES, they are now sometimes given independently.

Neville (b) French; 'new city'. Originally only a surname.

Nicholas (b) Greek; 'victory of the people'. St. Nicholas is the patron saint of children. *Dim.* NICK, NICKY. NICODEMUS is a variant of NICHOLAS.

Nigel (b) Latin; 'black'.

Nina (g) Originally a diminutive of ANNE, this name now stands alone, as also does NINETTE.

Ninian (b) Scottish; origin obscure.

Nita (g) Latin; 'bright, neat'. NETTA is also sometimes found. NITA is occasionally used as a diminutive of ANITA.

Noah (b) Hebrew; 'rest'.

Noel, Nowell (b and g) French; 'Christmas'.

Nona (g) Latin; 'the ninth child'. *Dim.* NONIE.

Nora, Norah (g) An Irish form of the Latin; 'honour'.

Norbert (b) Teutonic; 'Niord's brightness'.

Noreen (g) Diminutive of NORAH, q.v., but usually given independently.

Norma (g) Latin; 'square'—hence a norm. Originally popularised by Bellini's opera.

Norman (b) 'a Norwegian'. Until recently used mainly in Scotland. *Dim.* NORM.

OTTO

Obadiah (b) Hebrew; 'servant of the Lord'. *Dim.* OBIE.

Octavia (g) Latin; 'eighth child'. Name of the Emperor

Octavius

Augustus's sister, and of Octavia Hill, the nineteenth century social pioneer.

Octavius (b) Masculine equivalent of the above.

Odile (g) Teutonic; 'of the fatherland'. *Dim.* ODETTE, which is perpetuated in the principal dancer in the ballet "Swan Lake".

Olga (g) Slavonic; 'holy'.

Olive, Olave (g) One of the plant names.

Oliver (b) French; from the same root as the above. Its vogue was influenced by Oliver Cromwell. *Dim.* NOLL, NOLLIE, OLLY.

Olivia (g) Italian form of OLIVE. *Dim.* LIVIA, LIVY.

Ophelia (g) Greek; either from 'serpent' or from 'wisdom'. Rare in England but used occasionally due to Shakespeare's Ophelia, from "Hamlet".

Oriana (g) Latin; 'resurgent'. Originally a poetic name for Queen Elizabeth I, it was revived by Tennyson in his "Ballad of Oriana".

Orlando (b) Italian; 'fame of the land'. A romantic name which never quite died out, it was originally made known by Ariosto's "Orlando Furioso".

Orson (b) Italian; 'a bear'. Little used, but kept alive by the well-known actor of that name.

Osbert (b) Teutonic; 'divinely bright'. Made known in contemporary times by Sir Osbert Sitwell, the writer and man of letters.

Osborn (b) Teutonic; 'divine man'.

Oscar (g) Old English; 'divine spear'.

Osmund (b) Teutonic; 'divine protection'.

Osric (b) Teutonic; 'divine power'.

Oswald (b) Anglo-Saxon; 'free of hand'.

Otto (b) Teutonic; 'rich'. Often used formerly for members of the royal family in the Holy Roman Empire.

Owen (b) Origin uncertain, but it has been suggested that it comes from EUGENIUS; 'well born'. Now used in England as well as Wales.

P

PHILIP

Pain (b) Latin; 'rustic'. Now rare except as a surname. The root name, PAGAN, is sometimes found.

Pamela (g) Greek; 'all sweetness'. *Dim*. PAM.

Pascal (b) Greek; 'suffering', i.e. the suffering of Christ and thus chiefly used for children born at or around Easter.

Pascoe (b) Cornish variant of the above.

Patience (g) One of the abstract virtue names. *Dim*. PATTY, PAT.

Patricia (g) Latin; 'patrician'. *Dim*. PAT, PATYS, TRIC, TRICIA.

Patrick (b) Masculine equivalent of the above. Widely used, particularly in Ireland, where the diminutive PADDY is used generically for Irishmen as St. Patrick was the patron saint of Ireland. *Dim*. PAT, PADDY, PATE. PADRAIC is another and more Irish form.

Paul (b) Latin; 'small'. Universally popular, the name owes its popularity largely to St. Paul the Apostle, although there were very many minor saints of that name.

Paula (g) Feminine version of Paul.

Paulina, Pauline (g) Diminutives of Paula. PAULET is also occasionally found.

Pearl (g) One of the jewel-names.

Penelope (g) Greek; 'weaver'. The name of the beautiful wife of Ulysses who unpicked at night the robe she wove by day. *Dim*. PEN, PENNY.

43

Perceval

Perceval, Percival (b) French; 'pierce the vale'. *Dim.* PERCY, PERCE.

Percy (b) As well as being a diminutive of PERCIVAL, PERCY was an independent surname of one of the oldest English families, and thence became a Christian name on its own. It was one of the names of the poet Shelley. *Dim.* PERCE.

Peregrine (b) Latin; 'wanderer'. St. Peregrinus was an Irish prince who dwelt as a hermit in Italy.

Perdita (g) Latin; 'lost'. Made known in Shakespeare's "A Winter's Tale".

Perpetua (g) Latin; 'everlasting'. *Dim.* PET, PEPPI.

Peter (b) Greek; 'stone' or 'rock'. Name of St. Peter, who keeps the gates of Heaven, and in this connection is taken to mean 'foundation' of the Church. After him St. Peter's in the Vatican City is named, and this centre of the Roman Catholic Church bears the Latin inscription, 'Thou art *"petros"* (stone) and on this *"petra"* (rock) I will build my church!' The name was also borne by Peter the Great, after whom St. Petersburg, now Leningrad, was named. *Dim.* PETE.

Petronella, Petrina (g) Feminine versions of Peter, the former a diminutive of PETRONIA.

Phelim (g) Celtic; 'the ever good'. Seems now to be confined to Ireland.

Philemon (b) Greek; 'loving'.

Philetus (b) Greek; 'affection'.

Philibert (b) Teutonic; 'exceeding bright'.

Philip (b) Greek; 'fond of horses'. Name of the Apostle Philip, and of the royal families first of Macedon and later of Spain. *Dim.* PHIL, PIP.

Philippa (g) English feminine version of the above. *Dim.* PHIL, PIPPA, which was made known by Robert Browning in the poem "Pippa Passes".

Phineas (b) Celtic; 'whitehouse'. The name was kept alive by Anthony Trollope's "Phineas Finn".

Phoebe (g) Greek; 'radiant'. Phoebe was the Greek moon goddess. The name was popularised in England by Shakespeare.

Phyllida (g) A variant of Phyllis, q.v. *Dim.* PHYL.

Phyllis (g) Greek; 'a green leaf or bough'. The name was brought into use in England by the pastoral and lyric poets, with whom it was a favourite. *Dim.* PHYL, PHYLLIE.

Piers (b) An early English contraction of PETER, through the French. The earliest example is "Piers Ploughman".

Plaxy (g) Origin obscure; possibly Greek; 'active'. Now found mainly in Cornwall.

Placida (g) Latin; 'serene'.

Polly (g) Originally a diminutive of Mary, this name is now sometimes given independently. *Dim.* POL.

Poppy (g) One of the less common flower-names.

Portia (g) Latin; 'pig', but it was brought to popularity by the character of that name in Shakespeare's play "A Merchant of Venice".

Postumus (b) Latin; 'last'. Originally this name was given to children born after the death of their father, but it is now seldom used.

Primrose (g) One of the flower-names, but sometimes associated more with Botticelli's picture "Prima Vera" than with the flower.

Priscilla (g) Latin; 'of olden times'. *Dim.* Prissy.

Prosper (b) Latin; 'fortunate'. This name was used in the form of PROSPERO by Shakespeare, and is also found in France, but it is now rare in this country.

Prudence (g) Latin; 'prudent', thus one of the abstract virtue names. *Dim.* PRU, PRUE, PRUDIE.

Prunella (g) Old French; 'plum-coloured'. *Dim.* PRU.

Psyche (g) Greek; 'the spirit'. This name is kept alive by the myth of Cupid and Psyche, and the many paintings that have been done to illustrate it.

Q

QUEENIE

Queenie (g) There is no known origin for this name, unless it is a direct translation of the Latin Regina, 'queen'. Girls christened VICTORIA are sometimes called QUEENIE.

Quentin (b) Latin; 'the fifth child'. Almost all the numerals from one to ten have been used as Christian names at some time or other. Also spelt QUINTIN.

Quintella, Quintina (g) The feminine version of the above.

R

ROWENA

Rachel (g) Hebrew; 'a ewe'. Always a fairly popular name it was made more so by the great Franco-Jewish actress of tragedy. *Dim*. RACHIE.

Radegund (g) Old German; 'counsellor of war'.

Raine, Reine (g) French for 'queen'.

Ralph, Ralf, Rafe (b) From the Old English RADULF 'counsel of wolf'.

Randal (b) Derived from RANDOLPH, q.v. Sometimes spelt RANDLE. *Dim.* RAN.

Randolph, Randolf (b) Old English; 'house-wolf'. *Dim.* WOLF, RANDO, RANDY, RAN. Also frequently found as a surname.

Raoul (b) French form of RALPH, q.v. Occasionally given in this country, and is the source of a number of surnames beginning with RAW—.

Raphaela, Rafaelle, Rafaele (g) Hebrew; 'healed by God'. This name is associated both with the Archangel and also with the great Italian painter of the Renaissance.

Rastus (b) Greek; 'staunch'.

Ray (b) Originally the diminutive of RAYMOND, q.v., but now given independently. Also sometimes used for girls, perhaps as a diminutive for RACHEL.

Raymond (b) Old French; 'wise protection'. *Dim.* RAY.

Rebecca, Rebekah (g) Hebrew; 'a snare'. *Dim.* REBA, BECKY. The name of Daphne du Maurier's well-known heroine.

Redmond (b) Teutonic; 'counsel-protection'.

Regina (g) Latin; 'queen'. First used in the Middle Ages and may refer to the Virgin Mary, being the Queen of Heaven.

Reginald (b) Teutonic; 'judgement power'. *Dim.* REG, REGGIE.

Renè (b) French; 'born again'.

Renèe (g) Feminine version of the above and also the diminutive of IRENE.

Renfred (b) Old German; 'counsel of peace'. Now found mostly in Cornwall.

Reuben (b) Hebrew; 'behold a son'. Now mostly a Jewish name. *Dim.* REUB.

Rex (b) Latin; 'king'. Also sometimes used as a contraction of REGINALD.

Reynaud (b) Teutonic; 'hard counsel'.

Reynold (b) Old English; 'power and might'. Now usually a surname.

Rhea (g) Greek; mother of the gods.

Rhoda (g) Greek; 'a rose'. *Dim.* RHO, RHODIE.

Rhys (b) Welsh; 'impetuous'. Pronounced, and sometimes spelt REECE.

Richard (b) Old English; 'stern ruler'. A name borne by three remarkable English kings, including Richard Lion Heart. *Dim.* DICCON, DICK, DICKIE, RITCHIE.

Richenda (g) Old German; 'ruler'. Also used as a feminine version of Richard.

Rita (g) Originally a diminutive of MARGARITA, q.v. it has now become a name in its own right, and in recent years probably furthered by the Hollywood actress, Rita Hayworth.

Robert (b) Old German; 'bright fame'. Now mainly a Scottish name. *Dim.* RAB, RABBIE; (Scottish), ROB, ROBBIE, BOB, BOBBIE.

Roberta (g) Feminine version of the above. *Dim.* BOBBIE.

Robin (b) Originally a diminutive of ROBERT, ROBIN is now almost always used independently. The stories of Robin Hood and Robin Goodfellow have influenced its popularity in the past, as has Christopher Robin in modern times.

Robina, Robinette (g) Feminine versions of ROBIN, found mainly in Scotland.

Rodney (b) Old English; 'road-servant'. Originally a surname, RODNEY is now used as a Christian name.

Roderick (b) Old German; 'famous ruler'. *Dim.* RODDY, RORY.

Roderica (g) Feminine version of RODERICK.

Roger (b) Teutonic; 'spear of fame'. Borne by the famous Sir Roger de Coverley. *Dim.* RODGE.

Roland, Rowland (b) Teutonic; 'fame of the land'.

Name of the legendary subject of the "Chanson de Roland" of the times of Charlemagne. Roland is the French version of the Italian ORLANDO, and they were, in fact, the same person. *Dim.* ROLY.

Rolf, Rolfe, (b) A variant of RUDOLPH, q.v.

Rollo, (b) A contraction of RUDOLPH, q.v.

Roma (g) Latin; 'of Rome'.

Romeo (b) Contraction of ROMULUS, q.v. The name is rare, but kept alive by Shakespeare's "Romeo and Juliet".

Romola (g) Feminine version of ROMULUS, q.v.

Romulus (b) Diminutive of the Latin; 'of Rome'. The name owes its recognition solely to the well-known myth of the foundation of Rome by Romulus and Remus, who were brought up by a she-wolf.

Rona (g) Feminine version of Ronald, q.v.

Ronald (b) Scottish contraction of REGINALD, q.v. RANALD is also sometimes found. *Dim.* RON, RONNIE.

Rory, Rorie (b) Celtic; 'red, ruddy'. This is now almost entirely an Irish name.

Rosa (g) Latin; variant of Rose, q.v.

Rosabel, Rosalie, Rosina, Rosita, Rosanna, Rose-anne (g) All these are derived from ROSE, q.v.

Rosaline, Rosalind (g) Spanish; 'fair as a rose'. First used by Shakespeare in "As You Like It".

Rosamund (g) Probably Teutonic; 'horse-protection', rather than anything to do with ROSE.

Rose (g) Although the word comes from the Teutonic *hros* 'a horse' the name has been used for many centuries in its floral sense. *Dim.* ROSIE.

Rosemary (g) Name of the plant. Now the name, through the plant, is associated with Shakespeare's "There's rosemary, that's for remembrance", from "Hamlet".

Rowena (g) Celtic; 'white skirt'. This name became popular after the publication of Scott's "Ivanhoe".

Roy (b) Celtic; 'red', or possibly from French; 'king'.

Roxanna, Roxane (g) Persian; 'dawn'.

Ruby (g) One of the jewel-names.

Rudolph, Rudolf (b) Teutonic; 'wolf-fame'. *Dim.* DOLPH, DOLF, WOLF, RUDIE, ROLF.

Rue (g) Greek; from the herb plant 'rue'.

Rufus (b) Latin; 'red-haired'.

Rupert (b) Teutonic; 'bright fame'—the same as ROBERT. The name was introduced into England by Charles II's nephew, Prince Rupert, and has come to be associated with his rash brilliance.

Russell (b) Old French; 'red-head'. Now more common as a surname. *Dim.* RUSTY, RUSS.

Ruth (g) Hebrew; origin obscure. Possibly 'vision of beauty', or 'friend'. Sometimes given as an abstract virtue name, meaning 'pity, sympathy'. The name was first used in England after the Reformation, and has since been used steadily. It has been kept alive by various European poets, chiefly Victor-Hugo and Keats in his "Ode to a Nightingale". *Dim.* RUTHIE.

S

SARAH

Sabina, Sabine (g) Latin; 'a woman of the Sabine tribe'. Unfortunately associated with the well-known story of the rape of the Sabines.

Sabrina (g) Latinised name for the River Severn. First used by Milton for one of the nymphs in "Comus".

Sacha (b) Greek; 'helper of mankind'. From the same root, through the Russian, as ALEXANDER.

Sacheverell (b) Originally a surname, derived from the French village of St. Chevreuil-du-Tronchet. Borne by Sacheverell Sitwell, the writer. *Dim.* SACHIE.

Sadie (g) A diminutive of SARAH, q.v., but also sometimes given independently, particularly in America.

Sally (g) Also a diminutive of SARAH, q.v.

Salome (g) Hebrew; 'peace'. Not a common name, because of the biblical character, and Oscar Wilde's book on her.

Samson (b) Hebrew; 'child of the sun-god'. The name was made better known in England through Milton's "Samson Agonistes", and there was also a Celtic Bishop of that name who founded an abbey in Brittany. *Dim.* SAM.

Samuel (b) Hebrew; 'name of God'. Not known in England before the Reformation, and now very largely a Jewish name only, and also a surname. *Dim.* SAM.

Sanchia (g) Latin; 'holy'.

Sandra (g) Originally purely a diminutive of ALEXANDRA, it is now sometimes given independently.

Sandy (b) This diminutive of ALEXANDER is, like the above, now occasionally used by itself.

Sapphira (g) Either Greek; 'sapphire', or Hebrew; 'beautiful'.

Sarah, Sara (g) Hebrew; 'princess'. The wife of ABRAHAM was given this name by God instead of her former name, SARAI, 'the quarrelsome'. The name was not common in England until after the Reformation. *Dim.* SALLY, SADIE.

Sarita (g) Diminutive of SARAH, q.v. 'a little princess'.

Saul (b) Hebrew; 'the asked for'. Name of the first king of Israel and then of Saul of Tarsus. Not a common name in England, but kept alive by Robert Browning's long poem "Saul".

Scholastica (g) Latin; 'scholar'. St. Scholastica was the sister of St. Benedict.

Sean (b) Irish form of JOHN, q.v. Pronounced SHAWN.

Sebastian (b) Latin; 'man of Sebastia', or Greek; 'venerated'. The martyrdom of St. Sebastian who was shot to death with arrows, has been painted many times and keeps the name alive. The name was also used by Shakespeare. *Dim.* SEBA, BASTIAN, BASSY.

Sebastiana, Sebastienne (g) Feminine forms of the above.

Secundus (b) Latin; 'the second child'. The feminine form SECUNDA, is also occasionally found.

Selina (g) Latin; 'heaven'. SILLINA and CELINA are also found.

Selima (g) Hebrew; Feminine version of SOLOMON, q.v.

Selwyn (b) Old English; 'house-friend'. Now mainly used in Wales.

Septimus (b) Latin; 'the seventh child' The feminine form SEPTIMA is even rarer.

Seraphina (g) Latin; 'noble, burning'. SERAFITA is also sometimes found.

Serena (g) Latin; 'calm, serene'.

Serle (b) Old German; 'armed'. SEARLE is also found.

Seth (b) Hebrew; 'compensation'.

Seamus (b) Irish form of JAMES, q.v. Pronounced SHAMUS.

Sextus (b) Latin; 'sixth child'.

Sheila, Sheelagh (g) Originally the Irish form of CELIA, q.v., but now always an independent name.

Sheena (g) Irish form of JANE, q.v.

Shirley (g) Originally a surname which derived from the name of a place. Not a universal Christian name until the publication of Charlotte Brontë's novel "Shirley" in 1849. Further popularised by Hollywood film stars.

Sholto (b) Origin unknown.

Sibyl (g) Greek; ' a prophetess'. SIBYLLA and SIBILLE are also found. Name of one of Benjamin Disraeli's popular novels.

Sidney (b) Originally a surname, probably a contraction of St. Denis, and the name of the versatile Elizabethan Sir Philip Sidney. Now very common as a Christian name. *Dim.* SID.

Sidonia, Sidonie, Sidony (g) Latin; 'fine cloth'. Sometimes used, but usually with the spelling Sidonie, for example, Sidonie Goossens, the famous harpist.

Siegfried (b) Teutonic; 'victorious peace'. The name was popularised by Wagner's opera, but fell into total disuse in England with the 1939-45 war because of its German associations and the 'Line' of the same name. *Dim.* SIG, SIGGIE.

Silas (b) Contraction of SYLVANUS, q.v. Revived by George Eliot's novel "Silas Marner".

Silvester (b) Latin; 'of the forest'. A very common name in the Middle Ages. *Dim.* SIL.

Simeon (b) Hebrew; 'obedient'. Not to be confused with the following.

Simon (b) Greek; 'snub-nose'. *Dim.* SI.

Solomon (b) Hebrew; 'peaceable'. Now almost solely a Jewish name. *Dim.* SOL, SOLLY.

Sonia (g) Slavonic; 'wise'. A diminutive of the following:

Sophia, Sophy (g) Greek; 'wisdom'. Name of the famous church of St. Sophia at Constantinople.

Sorcha (g) Celtic; 'bright'.

Stacey, Stacy (b and g) English contraction of ANASTASIA, and ANASTASIUS.

Stanislas, Stanislaus (b) Slavonic; 'camp'. Chiefly

a Polish name associated with two Polish saints
of the Roman Catholic church. *Dim.* STAN.

Stanley (b) Like Howard and Percy, this was originally
an old English surname derived from a place-name.
Dim. STAN.

Stella (g) Latin; 'star'. It has long been popular, and
was first used in literature in Sir Philip Sidney's
sonnets "Astrophel to Stella". The name also has a
Roman Catholic association with "Stella Maris",
which is a title of invocation of the Virgin Mary.

Stephana, Stephanie (g) Feminine versions of
STEPHEN, q.v.

Stephen, Steven (b) Greek; 'crown'. In the Middle
Ages this was a favourite name for European royal
houses. STEPHEN was the name borne by the
first Christian martyr whose feast day is 26th Decem-
ber, Boxing Day. *Dim.* STEVE, STEEVIE.

Stewart, Stuart (b) Anglo-Saxon; 'a steward'. Although
still a popular Christian name it is also frequently
found as a surname.

Susan (g) Originally a contraction of SUSANNA, q.v.,
but now given independently. *Dim.* SUE.

Susanna (g) Hebrew; 'graceful white lily'. *Dim.* SUE,
SUKEY, SUSIE.

Suzanne (g) French version of SUSANNA.

Swain (b) Norse; 'strong'.

Sybil (g) Alternative but incorrect spelling of Sibyl, q.v.

Sylvanus (b) Latin; in the Latin classics SYLVANUS
was a deity of the fields and forests. It became a
popular name in England with the pastoral and lyric
poets of the sixteenth century.

Sylvester. See Silvester.

Sylvia (g) Latin; 'wood-dweller'. Often found in
pastoral stories and poems, the name was first made
known and is kept alive by Shakespeare's song in
"The Two Gentlemen of Verona", "Who is Sylvia,
What is She?" *Dim.* SYLVIE.

T

TRISTRAM

Tabitha (g) Aramaic; 'a gazelle'. Now a rare name, possibly due to its association with cats.

Tacita (g) Latin; 'the silent'.

Tace (g) English contraction of the above, now rare and found only among Quakers.

Tadhgh (b) Celtic; 'poet'. Pronounced THEAGUE.

Taffy (b) Originally a Welsh diminutive of David, but also given independently, and used generically for Welshmen.

Talbot (b) Old English; 'faggot-cutter'. This was originally a surname, but is now often given as a Christian name.

Tamsin (g) Contraction of THOMASINA, q.v. Now rare except in the West Country, particularly Cornwall. *Dim.* TAMSIE.

Tancred (b) Old German; 'grateful speech'.

Tatiana (g) The name of a third century martyr of the Orthodox Church, and consequently a favourite Russian name, but it is not often used in England.

Tanya (g) A contraction of the above, more common in England.

Terence (b) Latin; 'tender'. The name of a Roman writer of comedy, TERENCE has now a slightly Irish bias. *Dim.* TERRY.

Teresa, Theresa (g) Greek; 'reaper'. St. Teresa of

55

Avila in the sixteenth century, and St. Therese of
Lisieux in the nineteenth century have popularised
this name, particularly among Roman Catholics.
Dim. TERRY, TESS.

Tess, Tessa (g) Originally diminutive of TERESA,
these names are now sometimes given independently,
and their popularity was increased in modern times
by Hardy's novel "Tess of the d'Urbervilles".

Thaddeus (b) Greek; 'praise', although this etymology
is not certain. *Dim.* THADDIE, TADDY, TAD.

Thea (g) Greek; 'divine'.

Thekla (g) Greek; 'divine fame'.

Thelma (g) Origin obscure; the name was perhaps
invented by the novelist Marie Corelli, and is now
quite common in this country.

Theobald (b) Teutonic; 'folk-bold'. Now mainly found
as a surname. *Dim.* THEO.

Theodora (g) A feminine version of the following:

Theodore (b) Greek; 'God's gift'. *Dim.* THEO.

Theodoric (b) Teutonic; 'people's ruler'. *Dim.* THEO.

Theodosia (b) Greek; 'divinely given'. *Dim.* THEO,
DOSIA.

Theophilus (b) Greek; 'beloved of God'. *Dim.* THEO.

Thirzah (g) Hebrew; 'pleasantness'. This name was
very popular in England in the late eighteenth
century but is now rare.

Thomas (b) Aramaic; 'twin'. The popularity of this
name in England may be due to St. Thomas of
Canterbury (Thomas à Beckett) but before the
Norman conquest it was used only as a priest's
name. *Dim.* TOM, TOMMIE, TOMMY.

Thomasina (g) Feminine version of Thomas, q.v.

Thorold (b) Norwegian; 'Thor's rule'.

Thurlow (b) Teutonic; 'Thor's sport'. Now mainly
a surname.

Tibal, Tibble (b) English contraction of THEOBALD,
q.v.

Tiernan (b) Celtic; 'kingly'. Variants are TIERNAY, TIERNEY.

Tilda, Tilly (g) Contractions of MATILDA, q.v. These names are sometimes given independently.

Timothy (b) Greek; 'honouring God'. Name of the companion of St. Paul and was not commonly used in England until after the Reformation. *Dim.* TIM, TIMMY.

Timothea (g) Feminine version of TIMOTHY, q.v.

Tirconnel (b) Celtic; 'lord of the land'. This name is mainly found in Ireland, and is the origin of "Donegal".

Titus (b) Origin obscure, but perhaps Greek; 'I honour'. It was a common name in England after the Reformation, and has never quite died out.

Tobias (b) Hebrew; 'God is good'. *Dim.* TOBY.

Tobit, Tobin (b) Hebrew; 'Son of Tobias', but now often used as variants of TOBIAS. TOBIN is most common in Ireland.

Toby (b) Originally a diminutive of TOBIAS, and now used independently.

Toole (b) Celtic; 'lordly'. Now found almost solely in Ireland, often as a surname.

Tracey (g) Originally a contraction of TERESA, this name is more often found as a surname. It is also sometimes given to boys.

Trefor (b) Welsh form of Trevor, q.v.

Trevor (b) Originally a surname of considerable antiquity, this name is now often used as a Christian name, particularly in Ireland.

Tristram (b) Celtic; 'a herald'. Now a rare name in England but kept alive by the Arthurian myth of "Tristram and Isolde", and by the Wagnerian opera of that title.

Truda, Trudie (g) Diminutive of ERMENTRUDE, these names are occasionally given in this country.

Troth, Truth (g) One of the rarer abstract virtue names, which was frequently given in England in the seventeenth century.

Tryphaena, Tryphena (g) Greek; 'dainty'. This name was first popularised in England by the Puritans. *Dim.* TRIFFIE.

Tudor (b) Welsh contraction of THEODORE, q.v.

URSULA

U

Uchtred (b) Teutonic; 'mind council'. Now rare.

Ulick (b) Origin obscure. Possibly Danish; 'mind-reward', or else a doublet of Ulysses, q.v.

Ulric (b) Old English; 'wolf rule'.

Ulrica (g) Feminine version of the above.

Ulysses (b) Greek; 'the hater'. Latin name for the well-known Greek hero Odysseus, and revived, particularly in Ireland, in modern times by James Joyce's famous novel of that name.

Una, Oonagh (g) Latin; 'the one'. Name of the heroine of the Spencer's allegory "Faerie Queene".

Urban (b) Latin; 'of the town'. This was a very popular name in the mediaeval church, but is now rare.

Uriah (b) Hebrew; 'the Lord is my light'. This name has been besmirched by Dickens' odious character Uriah Heep in "David Copperfield".

Uriel (b) Hebrew; 'light of God'.

Urith (g) Meaning obscure, but the name was found often in seventeenth century England.

Ursula (g) Latin; 'little she-bear'. *Dim.* URSE, URSIE.

V

VIRGINIA

Valentine (b and g) Latin; 'strong'. St. Valentine was a Roman martyr whose feast day coincides with the old, and probably pagan custom of taking as true love the first person of the other sex met with on the morning of February 14th. *Dim.* VAL.

Valerian (b) Latin; 'strong', 'healthy'. *Dim.* VAL.

Valerie (g) French feminine form of the above. *Dim.* VAL.

Vanessa (g) Invented by Swift for Esther Vanhomrigh, and taken up by Hugh Walpole.

Vanora (g) Celtic; 'white wave'. The Scottish variant of Guinevere.

Vashti (g) Persian; 'star'. Found mostly in Cornwall. *Dim.* VASSY.

Venetia (g) Celtic; 'blessed', but more often given under the impression that it refers to Venice. Name of one of Benjamin Disraeli's novels.

Vera (g) Latin; 'true'.

Verena (g) German; 'true picture', and the name of a virgin martyred under Diocletian and much venerated in Switzerland.

Verity (g) One of the abstract virtue names.

Vernon (b) Latin; 'flourishing'. Also common as a surname. *Dim.* VERN.

Veronica (g) Latin; compound of 'true' and 'of an

image'. The legend of St. Veronica's handkerchief which supposedly retained the image of Christ's face after having been used to cover it, was a favourite subject for religious painting.

Vesta (g) Latin; 'a hearth'. The Vestal Virgins in ancient Rome were priestesses of a rigorous order who tended an eternal flame.

Victor (b) Latin; 'victorious'. It has never been very popular in this country.

Victoria (g) Latin; 'victory'. The name did not become popular in this country until the reign of Queen Victoria who was the first well-known person to bear the name, but it is now frequently found. The French and Italian versions of the name were found earlier but were derived from the third century Roman martyr, Victoria. *Dim.* VICK, VICKY.

Victorine (g) French diminutive of VICTORIA.

Vida, Vidette (g) Welsh feminine form of David, q.v.

Vincent (b) Latin; 'conquering'. Name of a number of saints and martyrs, particularly St. Vincent de Paul, a French seventeenth century social worker, *Dim.* VIN, VINNY.

Viola (g) Latin; 'violet', from the Italian. Its popularity is probably due to Shakespeare's "Twelfth Night". VIOLETTA is also found occasionally. *Dim.* VI.

Violet (g) English version of VIOLA, and more common in this country, and especially in Scotland. *Dim.* VI.

Virgil (b) Latin; 'flourishing'. Now rare but very common in England in the seventeenth century when the works of the poet Virgil were first known.

Virginia (g) Latin; 'of spring'. *Dim.* VIRGIE, GINNY.

Vivian (b) Latin; 'alive'. Also spelt VIVYAN, VYVYAN. *Dim.* VIV.

Vivien (g) Feminine version of the above. VIVIENNE is also found.

Voleta, Voletta (g) Old French; 'veiled'.

W

WARREN

Walburga (g) Anglo-Saxon; 'powerful protection'.

Waldo (b) Norse; 'power'.

Wallace (b) Originally a Scottish surname, but now used universally as a Christian name. *Dim*. WAL, WALLY.

Walter (b) Old German; 'folk-ruler'. *Dim*. WAL, WALT WALLY.

Waltheof (b) Old English; 'thief-rule'.

Wanda (g) Old German; 'stem', 'stock'.

Warner (b) Teutonic; 'protecting warrior'. Now more usually found as a surname.

Warren (b) Teutonic; 'protecting friend'. Now more common as a surname.

Washington (b) Originally a surname derived from a place-name, it is now given as a Christian name, particularly in America in honour of George Washington, the President of the United States who, it is said, could not tell a lie.

Wendy, Wenda (g) Teutonic; 'wanderer'. WENDY was popularised by Barrie's "Peter Pan and Wendy".

Wilfred (b) Anglo-Saxon; 'resolute peace'. *Dim*. WIL, WILF.

Wilhelmina (g) Feminine version of WILLIAM, originally German and Dutch, and still not common in this country. *Dim*. WILLA, MINA, MINNA

William (b) Teutonic; 'helmet of resolution'. The name was introduced into England in the eleventh century and is still one of the most popular boys' names. *Dim.* BILL, BILLIE, BILLY, WILL, WILLIE, WILLY.

Willis (b) A derivative of WILLIAM, q.v. this name is now mostly found as a surname.

Wilmot (b) Teutonic; 'resolute mood', originally used for both sexes.

Winifred, Winfred (g) Celtic; 'white wave', and thus connected to GUINEVERE and its derivatives. *Dim.* WIN, WINNIE.

Winne (g) Celtic; 'white'.

Winston (b) Originally a place name, this name was used in the Churchill family since the seventeenth century. During and after the 1939-45 war this name was given to a large number of children in honour of Sir Winston Churchill, and is now an accepted boys' name in England. *Dim.* WINNIE.

Winthrop (b) Teutonic; 'friendly village'. Mainly a surname but occasionally used as a Christian name in this country, and frequently in America.

X

Xavier (b) Arabic; 'splendid'. Now rare in this country, but it is still used in France and among Catholics to commemorate St. Francis Xavier, a sixteenth century Spanish missionary who went to the Far East.

Xenophon (b) Greek; 'strange voice'. Name of the Athenian historian and general of the fourth century B.C.

Xerxes (b) Persian; 'king'. Name of the young Persian king in the fifth century B.C.

Y

YVONNE

Yolande (g) Perhaps an old French derivative of VIOLA, q.v. and a doublet of IOLANTHE, q.v. Not a common name, but kept alive by the film industry.

Yorick (b) Originated by Shakespeare in "Hamlet"—"Alas, poor Yorick"—the name was probably a phonetic rendering of the Danish GEORG, and was later taken up by Sterne in his "Sentimental Journey."

Yvonne (g) French feminine diminutive of YVES, which is the Breton form of EVAN, and hence JOHN, q.v. The form YVETTE is also occasionally found.

ZOE

Z

Zachariah (b) Hebrew; 'God has remembered'.

Zackary (b) English contraction of ZACHARIAH. *Dim.* ZACK, ZACKY.

Zedekiah (b) Hebrew; 'God is righteousness'.

Zenobia (g) The name of a famous Queen of Palmyra of Arabian birth who was eventually captured by Aurelian in A.D. 272. The name is now sometimes found in Cornwall, and was at one time a fashionable name of the exotic type.

Zilla, Zillah (g) Hebrew; 'shadow'. Now mainly a gypsy name.

Zita (g) Origin obscure.

Zoe (g) Greek; 'life'. Its use in England is fairly recent, but it was the name of a third century Roman martyr.

Zona (g) Greek; 'girdle'. More popular in America.

Zora (g) Arabic; 'dawn'. Found chiefly in Australia.

Zoroaster (b) Persian; 'golden star'. Zoroaster was the founder of a Persian religion a thousand years B.C. which had its basis in the sanctity of fire.

Zuleika (g) Arabic; 'fair'. Introduced into England by Max Beerbohm in his brilliant story "Zuleika Dobson".

Impreso en los Talleres de EDITORIAL FHER, S. A.
Calle Villabaso, 9.— BILBAO-ESPAÑA

PRINTED IN SPAIN